To Sally

with love

from Kathy

Summer 1978

D1538752

WALDOBORO
PUBLIC LIBRARY

MUSK OXEN

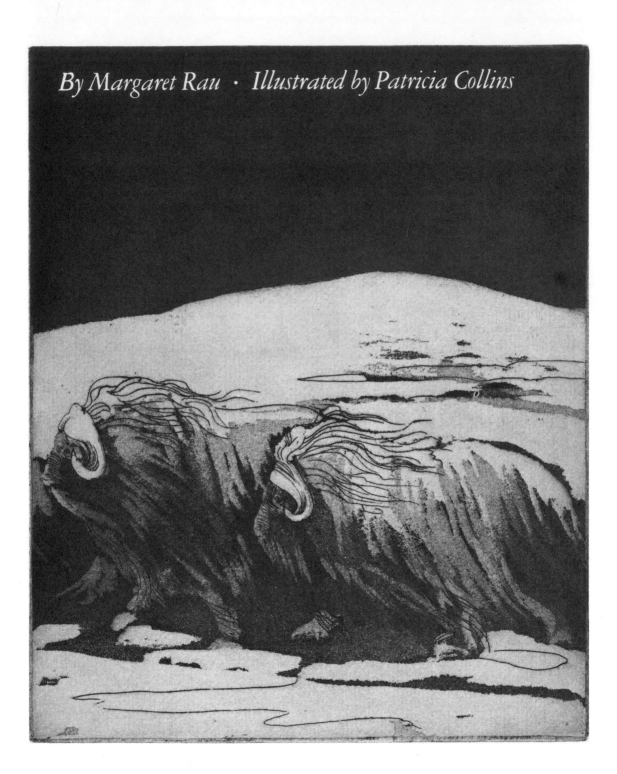

By Margaret Rau · Illustrated by Patricia Collins

MUSK OXEN

Bearded Ones of the Arctic

Thomas Y. Crowell Company · New York

For my second godson,
Jamie Auyong

Copyright © 1976 by Margaret Rau. Illustrations copyright © 1976 by Patricia Collins.
All rights reserved. Except for use in a review, the reproduction or utilization of this
work in any form or by any electronic, mechanical, or other means, now known or
hereafter invented, including xerography, photocopying, and recording, and in any
information storage and retrieval system is forbidden without the written permission of
the publisher. Published simultaneously in Canada by Fitzhenry & Whiteside Limited,
Toronto. Designed by Harriett Barton. Manufactured in the United States of America.

Library of Congress Cataloging in Publication Data
Rau, Margaret. Musk oxen: bearded ones of the Arctic. SUMMARY: Introduces the
physical characteristics, habits, and environment of an arctic animal that spends the long
northern winter entirely in the open. 1. Musk ox—Juv. lit. [1. Musk ox]
I. Collins, Patricia. II. Title.   QL737.U53R38   599'.7358   75-26538
ISBN 0-690-01040-0 (CQR)

1   2   3   4   5   6   7   8   9   10

MUSK OXEN

Winter is a desolate time in the cold northern regions of Greenland that lie above the Arctic Circle. During these months the sun never rises. The land is steeped in darkness, lighted only by the stars and moon and, occasionally, by the multicolored halos of the aurora borealis.

As early as the last days of October the sun has disappeared from the sky and the long polar night has begun. A thick blanket of snow covers the undulating, treeless plains, called tundra, over which the musk oxen roamed and grazed in summertime. Ice two feet thick binds the bays and the steep, craggy inlets, or fiords. Only the bony ridges of the mountains are bare, swept clean of snow by freezing gales howling over Greenland's perpetual inland icecap.

The icecap was formed about 500,000 years ago when the earth turned colder. Then a great ice sheet covered all Greenland. Today the ice has melted from around the edges of the island, but the central plateau still wears its thick cap of ice, which in places is several thousand feet deep.

It seems impossible that any living thing could endure this arctic land in winter. Yet life is here, most of it tucked away out of harm's reach. The white arctic hares are on the snowswept higher ridges, hiding in deep clefts in the rocks and coming out only to feed on the lichen growing there.

The little lemmings and the ermines, in their white winter coats, hide in the snug burrows they have dug for themselves in the snow. The female polar bears are also holed up in their snow dens waiting for the birth of their young, while the male bears wander over the icepack looking for seals for food. The seals live under the pack, but occasionally to get a breath of air they pop their heads up through holes they have made in the ice. It is then that the bears can grab them.

However, in the fiercest weather the bear forgets about food and digs himself a snow shelter wherever he happens to be, and there he waits out the storm. The arctic wolves and foxes who continually roam the country in search of food take refuge in snow dens too.

The musk ox, the largest land mammal of the arctic, braves the long northern winter entirely in the open. Musk oxen are equipped for cold. These huge animals weigh some eight to nine hundred pounds and stand about four and a half feet tall at the shoulder. Formidable curved horns sprout from a thick bony shield that protects the forehead.

They look much larger than they actually are because their squat, stocky bodies are covered with a thick coat of brown hair that hangs from the back, forming a long skirt that reaches to their white ankles. Even the tail and muzzle are covered with

hair, and a long beard hangs from the jowls. A lighter-brown frizzled mane sprouts from the nape of the neck and along the shoulders. Under the outer shawl of hair grows a thick inner coat of soft fur that makes for good protection against the cold.

"Musk ox" is a strange name for this animal, which is not an ox and has no musk glands. Even its scientific name, *Ovibos moschatus,* is inaccurate. *Moschatus* is Latin for "musk." *Ovibos* is Latin for an imaginary creature that is half sheep and half cattle. But the musk ox is not related to either of these animals. Zoologists who have studied its blood chemistry say it belongs to the goat family. Like the goat, it has a complex stomach capable of making good use of everything it eats. After feeding, it brings up the food, or cud, from the first part of the stomach to chew on it again. An animal that chews its cud like this is called a ruminant.

The musk ox has other goatlike characteristics also, such as its short tail and the way it can stand on its hind legs to browse on grass growing in rocky clefts. And it can scale almost sheer precipices with the agility of a goat.

Yet a musk ox can move more swiftly than any goat. Although with its short legs and heavy body it is no match for the swift wolf, it can easily outdistance a man. Some zoologists believe that it belongs in a family of its own, lying somewhere between the fleet-footed antelope and the sure-footed goat.

How did the musk ox get such an inappropriate name? It began back in 1689, when the animal was first mentioned by a

4

white man, a Canadian named Henry Kelsey. To him it looked like a sheep and a bison combined, so he called it an ox-sheep.

In 1814, more than a hundred years later, Henri Marie Ducrotay de Blainville, the French zoologist, was sent a single musk ox skin from Canada and asked to classify it. After examining this skin, de Blainville agreed with Kelsey and gave it the Latin name *Ovibos*. He added *moschatus* because he was told the animal gave off a musky scent and therefore must have musk glands. For a while it was believed that musk could be extracted from the musk ox just as it is from the musk deer.

However, the musk ox has no musk glands and can't produce musk. The idea probably sprang up because during the mating season the bulls give off a pungent odor, mistaken for musk by those who smelled it. At all other times of the year the musk ox is odorless. The Eskimos have a much better name for it— Oomingmak, meaning "Bearded One."

The musk ox comes of an ancient race. About a million years ago its ancestors were roaming the arctic wastes of North Central Asia. When the First Ice Age converted so much water into ice that the levels of the oceans were lowered, a long bridge of land appeared uniting Asia with Alaska. Some of the musk oxen crossed over this bridge into the arctic regions of North America. They were probably much larger than the musk oxen of today. The bones of one species found in Alaska show that it was a gigantic animal.

Musk oxen lived in the far north until the glaciers of the most recent ice age started spreading southward some 75,000 years ago. The animals moved just ahead of the ice sheet, browsing along its foot until they reached what had formerly been a warm climate. In North America they came as far south as Iowa and New York. In Europe they reached present-day Germany and France.

Here the musk oxen met prehistoric man for the first time. Drawings in the cave homes of these early men show how important the musk ox became to them. The flesh was sweet and good, and the thick hair coat provided fine protection against a climate suddenly grown very chilly. Hunters killed great numbers of the animals.

Some 30,000 years ago, when the climate warmed again and the glaciers began to retreat, the wholesale slaughter had wiped out the musk ox from Europe and Asia. The North American herds made their way back to the Arctic. Some went to Alaska, others to the Barren Grounds—dry, frigid plains in northern Canada. Many went to the offshore islands, including Greenland, probably crossing over ice to reach them.

Winter has always been a season of hunger for musk oxen. Their hoofs are not strong enough to dig through deep snow or break the ice to get at buried vegetation. So for their wintering grounds they have to migrate to the windswept ridges, which have only a sparse covering of arctic grasses and dwarf willow trees, their favorite food.

LACY SIMONS
OWNER & OPERATOR

316 MAIN STREET
ROCKLAND, ME 04841

In the short fall days individual musk ox herds gather on these ridges. There are bulls hoary with age and others just coming into maturity. There are cows, with smaller horns and narrower forehead shields. And there are calves, born the previous May, still wearing their short, woolly gray coats and suckling their mothers. Although the musk ox cow does not have much milk, what she does give is rich and good.

Through the long polar night the musk oxen stay on the ridges, grazing in tightly knit masses. When the gales blow their fiercest, spewing sleet and snow, the great, shaggy creatures crowd even more closely together for warmth, in triangular formation. At the point of the triangle, facing into the gale, stand the great bulls, whose humped shoulders help to ward off the wind. Behind the old bulls, the cows and young bulls form the three sides of the triangle. In the center, protected by all the bulky bodies, stand the woolly calves. Without this shelter they would die of cold, for their short coats can't keep them warm enough in such freezing weather.

At last, in the first week of February, the sun appears again. Hanging just above the horizon, it sends its long beams streaming over the frozen wastes of sea and land. There will still be many days of storm and thick gray fog ahead. But the returning light brings the promise of a gentler time.

Bit by bit, as the days progress and the sun climbs above the horizon, the snow starts to melt on the higher mountain slopes.

And the musk oxen are able to roam farther and farther away from their limited forage ground on the ridges.

Once again they break up into individual herds, each one led by an old bull. Some of the herds are small, made up of two or three cows and several calves and immature bulls. Other herds may contain as many as twenty-two to thirty animals.

The herds aren't permanent. Sometimes a larger herd breaks up into several smaller ones. Sometimes smaller herds join together to form a larger one. But there is never more than one old bull leader to each herd.

This bull takes authority when attack threatens. During peaceful times a cow with her calf in tow becomes the actual leader. She picks out the best pasture lands and chooses routes that her calf can easily follow. The other cows and calves come after her. The young bulls fan out on either side. The old bull leader takes up the rear, ambling along some fifty to one hundred yards behind the herd. Here he can keep a watchful eye on everything.

As they travel sedately along, the musk oxen appear very dignified. But they can be playful too. After grazing, the adults like to stretch out on their sides on a nearby snowdrift and go to sleep. When they waken they lie there calmly chewing their cud, their full bellies rumbling now and then with contentment.

Meanwhile the young calves are frisking about. Their favorite game is King of the Castle. One clambers to the top of a mound, looks around triumphantly, and paws the ground. That's a challenge to the others to rush it, butting with their hornless foreheads. Whoever is able to knock the calf off the mound becomes King of the Castle and has to hold its place against the others.

Butting is a favorite pastime with all the musk oxen. Not one of them will refuse the challenge to go a few rounds even though the other may be much bigger and stronger. But nobody gets hurt because it's just a game.

The musk oxen, however, can't play their games for long before becoming overheated in their heavy, shaggy coats. They aren't able to cool off by perspiring because they have only two sweat glands in their whole body. These glands are in the hind feet.

Whether browsing or resting or playing, the herd usually sticks together. But sometimes one of the calves becomes startled and runs away. Separated from the others, its instincts will carry it over a wide, circular course of two or three miles before leading it back to the herd. The herd knows the calf will return if possible and waits patiently for several hours. But if it isn't back by that time, the others will give up hope and move on.

The calf is in real danger out on its own. Wolves, ancient enemy of the musk ox, can make a quick kill of such a helpless creature. A male wolf can even bring down a full-grown musk ox bull.

Such a fight looks very unmatched. There stands the musk ox, several times bigger than the gaunt wolf. The musk ox swings his formidable horns to and fro trying to gore the other animal. But the wolf dances about just out of reach, searching for an opening.

Taking his time, knowing that the musk ox will eventually tire, the wolf usually aims for the head. At last he sees his chance and darts in. He manages to tear out a chunk of flesh including an eye. Streaming blood and blinded, the musk ox continues to swing his horns. But he can't see clearly and the wolf again dashes in, this time making for the throat. In less than an hour from the time the fight began, the musk ox is dead.

Of course sometimes the musk ox wins and gores the wolf. But if a pack of wolves is attacking a single musk ox, it hasn't a chance. It can't outrun the wolves because it becomes too overheated to keep up its first burst of speed. Its only protection is to stick with its fellows.

Over the centuries musk oxen have developed a fine defense against their old enemy. When the herd first sights wolves, it takes to flight to gain a little time and perhaps a better terrain. Then the bull leader marshals it into fighting position. If there's a cliff or steep bank nearby, he lines his company along it so that the animals won't be attacked from the rear. When the wolves approach, they find themselves facing a formidable array of horns.

If the terrain is open, the musk oxen form a circle with the bulls on the outside and the cows and calves in the center. Facing outward, the bulls stand with their hindquarters pressed together. The wolves are brought up short by that solid line of defense. But they don't give up. Yapping and dancing about, they keep looking for an opening to sneak in and snatch a calf. The old bull leader doesn't intend to let them do this. He snorts and rubs his horns with the inner sides of his front legs. This starts a secretion of fatty liquid flowing from small glands just below his eyes. The liquid spreads over the long hair that covers his face and keeps it from blowing over his eyes.

Now he makes a sortie that takes him some ten or twelve yards away from the circle. Head lowered, horns bent between his forelegs, he tries to catch a wolf off guard. If he can, he gores it and tosses it through the air so that it lands either badly torn or with its back broken.

Then, before he grows tired or winded, the old bull rushes back to his place in the circle and the bull on his left takes his turn. So it goes, round after round. If one of the musk oxen, even the leader, is killed or badly wounded, the others go on fighting. If necessary the cows take a turn too. But not one of the animals breaks rank until the wolves are killed or driven off.

Other dangers besides wolves await the herd on its leisurely trek down to the tundra plains. There are steep precipices slick with ice. Though musk oxen are among the most sure-footed of animals, even they can sometimes slip and fall to their death. So at such dangerous places the cow who has been leading waits until the old bull leader arrives. He picks the way down. But the cow won't follow him until she sees him reach bottom safely. Even then she may sometimes feel the route he has chosen is too steep for her calf, and will look about for an easier way over which she can nudge it along.

With the beginning of April the first of the migratory birds, the snow bunting, appears. Its song sounds over the high, cold Arctic, promising the coming spring. It is followed by the snowy owl and the raven that have been wintering in southern Greenland.

This is the mating season for many arctic animals, among them the lemming. The thick snow that still blankets the plains and deep valleys is pierced with thousands of tiny holes. Still in their white winter coats, the lemmings are wakening from their winter sleep and breaking out of their burrows to go in search of mates. Before the year is over each pair will have raised five litters of young.

The arctic hares, the great polar bears, the foxes and ermines, are entering their mating season too. And it is the time the musk ox cows bear the young they have carried through the long fall and winter months.

The calving period lasts on into June, and the calves that are born latest are the luckiest. Those that arrive in April have the

most difficult time because the weather is still so bleak. They would never survive if they were not born with their thick coat of gray wool. Weighing only twenty or so pounds, they look tiny and helpless among the herd of great animals. Even the yearling calves are now huge fellows weighing as much as two hundred pounds.

But the newborn calves gather strength rapidly. They are able to stand up in less than half an hour. Fifteen minutes after that they are suckling their mothers. And in two or three days they can travel with the herd.

Not many calves are born to each herd in the high Arctic. In some herds there may not be a single one. The number of calves depends on how well the cows were able to feed during the previous year's mating season. If the forage is poor, the cows will not become pregnant. And since the forage is seldom abundant, most musk ox cows in the wild bear only every other year, if then.

As April turns into May the musk oxen start shedding their inner wool. Gradually, thick tufts of it work up through the coarse outer coat of hair, which is permanent. The gray wool that is being shed forms a fleecy shawl over the outer coat and hangs from it in tassels. To rid themselves of it, the musk oxen rub themselves vigorously against great rocks or blocks of ice. Their trail is now marked by the discarded tufts, which cling to the dwarf willow branches or, blown by the wind, roll over the tundra in fluffy bundles. The wool will serve as good nesting material for the birds that are arriving now in numbers to rear their young. These are the great sea birds that travel northward over the oceans every year to have their families in the short summer of the Arctic Circle.

The air is filled now with honking and harsh cries and mewing as Brant geese, barnacle geese, eider ducks, and gulls fly in, many of them from far away. Last of all to arrive is the little arctic tern, a mighty traveler that spends seven months of every year on the wing. Its other home is Antarctica, some eight to ten thousand miles away.

With the spring the days grow longer, bringing more and more hours of light, and by mid-May the great thaw begins. It reaches its peak when June ushers in the long polar day of the Arctic Circle. Just as the sun never rose during the winter months, it will not set for the summer, though it will never rise very high above the horizon. But the constant daylight is enough to melt the winter's snow and ice. Water comes rushing down the mountains in torrents, bringing with it huge chunks of soil and stone. Rivers overflow their banks, and the low-lying land is flooded. Large gaps appear in the ice floor that covers the fiords and the river mouths, and the frozen earth turns into marsh around the lakes.

Looking across the tundra now, with its streams of hurrying water, its quiltwork arrangement of ponds and lakes, you would

never guess that this land is desert. Most of us think of deserts as very hot places. Actually a desert can be cold as well as hot. But it is always a place which has little precipitation. And here in northeastern Greenland there is less than ten inches of it a year.

The musk ox is, therefore, a desert creature. In warm, moist weather its coat would become a death trap because it's not water repellent. Heavy rains or snows can soak it thoroughly.

The musk ox is unable to lick itself dry as do the arctic wolf and fox. If a freeze quickly follows wet weather, icicles form in the long, thick hair. Unlike the wolf and fox, the musk ox can't bite off the icicles. It has to carry them around, tinkling at every step.

If another rain and freeze come, the icicles are enlarged. Sometimes they become as big as baseball bats or even form ice shields over the backs of the musk oxen. If a sudden freeze catches the musk ox while it is lying down, its coat can become matted to the ground. Then the animal will be unable to stir at all. Either way, it can't forage or fight off attacks by a wolf or polar bear. In recent years a warming trend with more rainfall in Greenland has caused the death of many musk oxen living in the southern limits of their territory.

Though there isn't much rainfall on the tundra, there is enough ground water to bring up vegetation in profusion. Plants grow quickly in the Arctic because of the perpetual summer daylight. The dwarf willows put out new leaves and branches that form a thick ground cover. They cannot strike deep roots, however, because even in summer the ground never thaws below the surface soil. With only shallow roots the trees can't grow tall. They never reach more than six inches in height, though some may be over a hundred years old.

Plains, slopes, and valleys are clothed with a mantle of lush blue-green grass. Tiny flowers bloom everywhere. Buttercups and arctic poppies add splashes of golden color. Saxifrage covers the hills with a purple sheen. And bees and other insects, even butterflies, flit over the flowers.

Everywhere the birds are busy with their nesting—purple sandpipers in the sedge along thawing streams, squaw ducks and red phalaropes in the marsh, gulls in inaccessible cliffs. High overhead floats the great snowy owl, so white against the pale arctic sky he looks like a ghost, accented by a big black beak and two dark, slitted eyes. His nest is on a mound in the marsh, and he has seven young to feed. Now and again he will swoop down to snatch up some careless young chick or lemming that has strayed.

The lemmings have changed their coats to russet brown to blend with the vegetation, but the owl has no trouble spotting them. There are thousands of them, and they supply food not only for the great snowy owl but also for the fierce skua gulls, the ravens, and the foxes. Foxes and wolves and owls are feeding on the arctic hares and on their young too. The hares pop up

24

everywhere as though by magic. And they're easily seen because their white coats never change.

It is a time of bounty for the musk oxen and the caribou, which share the same grazing grounds. The musk oxen have lost their gaunt look and are growing sleek and fat. Soon they will be entering their mating season, which falls in July and August.

A great difference comes over the bulls at this time. They begin emitting the distinctive odor that gave them their name. And they are no longer quiet and gentle.

The leaders strut around their herds stiff-legged with their heads cocked to one side. Now and then they let out a low growl. One by one they begin mating with the cows in their harem. They know when each cow is ready for mating because then she too gives off an odor, which the bull is quick to detect.

The first to mate are the young heifers, who at three years of age have just reached maturity. But before the mating, the bull and cow go through a curious ceremony. She runs. He chases her, and overtakes her. They have a mild butting contest. Off she runs again. He chases her again. At last the mating takes place.

But the leader has more to do than mate with the cows. He has to stand guard over his harem and be ready to meet the challenges of other bulls, who come to try to take away the herd from him. He has to fight each one in turn. The battles aren't like the friendly contests that have been going on during the rest of the year. These are fierce duels to prove which bull is the stronger. They follow a kind of ritual.

There stands a grizzled old leader, a battle-scarred veteran of some fifteen years. He faces an eight-year-old challenger. Both bulls raise their heads and press their muzzles against their chests, making an arch of neck and shoulders. This thrusts forward the shield of bone across their foreheads. Now they begin to circle round and round.

Suddenly the old bull snorts loudly. He bends his head and rubs his nose fiercely against a front leg. The younger bull answers with a snort, and he too bends his head and rubs his nose on his leg.

Then the two begin circling again, wagging their heads from side to side. At last when they are some seventy-five feet apart they halt, facing each other. Each utters one last loud snort and a bellow. They rush at each other headlong—but not to do any goring. It's a butting contest.

The galloping hoofs thunder over the earth at forty miles an hour. Crash! The thick, horned foreheads meet in a grinding racket. The two bulls shake their heads, dazed. They back away. There's another headlong rush, another crash.

And once again. Rush! Crash!

On the fourth rush the young bull's confidence leaves him. At the last minute he veers away from the crash and slinks off in shame. But though he has lost this battle, he won't give up so

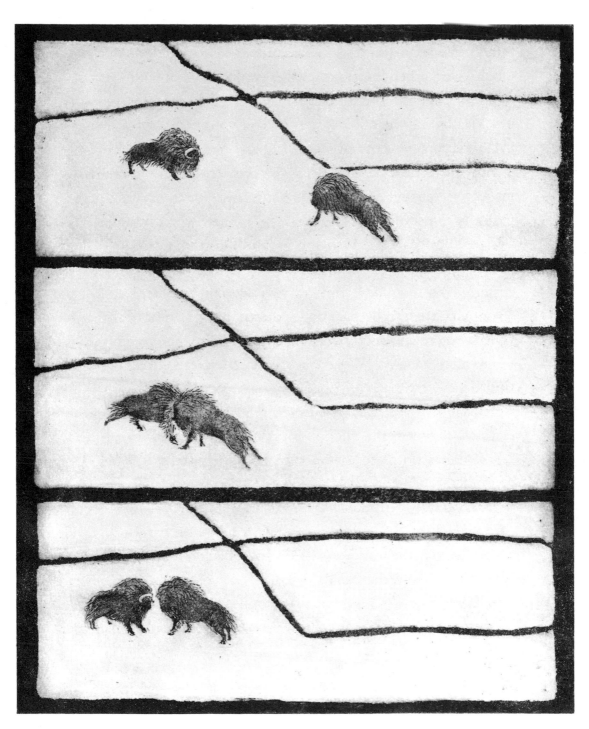

long as the mating season continues. He will look for other herds and other leaders to challenge. Perhaps he will eventually find one he can overthrow.

Meanwhile the old leader will have to meet more challengers. The next one is only five years old and has just become an adult, with horns now completely developed. He's still not nearly big or strong enough to tackle the old leader, but the mating urge in him is too strong. He doesn't veer from that first head-on crash. It sends him toppling to the ground, dead of a fractured skull.

Other challengers take his place. Day after day of challenges; the old bull has little time to rest or even eat. He is no longer young enough to bear up under the strain of so much fasting. He grows more and more weary and his movements become slower and more labored. When the last challenger comes, he knows he's met his match. Though he snorts and paws the ground menacingly, he feels deep inside a gnawing doubt that grows and grows. Right in the middle of his headlong rush he veers away.

There is no place in the herd for him now. He wanders off across the plain.

Very rarely will a defeated leader be able to muster enough confidence to make another challenge and gain back a herd. He may live out the rest of his life in solitude and die of old age. But it's more likely that he'll be killed by wolves or a polar bear.

Perhaps he'll join a group of other single bulls. There are many such groups. They too have an acknowledged leader, usually an older, experienced bull who musters them into the defense position when wolves attack. The bachelor bulls get along very well together during most of the year. But at the mating season the old instincts rise, and they challenge and battle one another as though there were a herd to win.

August brings real summer to the Arctic. Skies are often clear now and the temperature may rise to the forties and, on rare occasions, the fifties. The fiords and bays are free of ice except for occasional icebergs brought down by the polar currents. All the same, the short summer season is actually drawing to its close. The nights are growing longer and longer, the days shorter. The plants have passed their flowering and, as August enters September, begin to wither and die in the increasing night frosts.

Animals are molting in secret places. The musk ox yearlings are sprouting the coat of long hair that they will carry with them all their lives. The migratory birds are beginning to take their leave.

Summer ends abruptly. The temperature begins falling below the freezing mark. Snow squalls burst across the land and grow fiercer with the passing of September. Once more the musk oxen begin their trek to the old gathering grounds. Another bleak winter will soon be upon them.

For thousands of years musk oxen were able to live out the cycle of the year undisturbed in the lonely arctic wilderness. Their only enemies were the polar and grizzly bears and the

wolves. Wolves were the real menace then because they were far more numerous and hunted in great packs. But the defense the musk oxen had worked out protected them well.

Humans were there too—Eskimos living in scattered settlements—but they had only primitive spears. They much preferred hunting seals and seldom tackled Oomingmak.

But when the first white explorers came to the Arctic with guns and ammunition, man became the musk ox's worst enemy. The explorers found that the musk ox was a good source of food. Using huskies in place of wolves, they would set the fierce dogs on the musk oxen. When the musk oxen took up their defensive position to fight off the dogs, the men shot them down easily. Bull after bull fell. The others, bewildered, continued to defend in place of their fallen comrades until the last cow and calf were killed. The explorers shot down so many herds to supply themselves for the winter that they called it the "autumn slaughter."

Presently Eskimos began acquiring guns, and they too started shooting the musk oxen for their flesh and their warm coats. Big-game hunters, hearing tales that the creature of the north was the world's most dangerous animal, came to the Arctic to hunt it. They too had to gun down a whole herd before they could bring home a single pelt as trophy.

The musk ox could not survive such slaughter. By 1850 Eskimos had wiped out the last herd in Alaska. In Greenland and

Canada the killing continued, and was spurred on when at the beginning of the 1900's musk ox carriage robes became popular. Some 10,000 animals lost their lives to provide these robes.

The world's zoos also played an unknowing but important part in the destruction of the musk ox. They were so eager to get one for their collection of animals that they would pay a high price for it. Norwegian sealers and whalers found they could augment their incomes by shooting down a herd to capture a few of the docile little calves.

Finally in the 1920's, the Canadian government acted to give protection to the herds in its territory. In the next decade Denmark, which governs Greenland, followed suit. The zoos cooperated by refusing to buy any more musk oxen, discouraging would-be poachers. Gradually the musk oxen increased in number. And today they have reached their former population of some 12,000 animals in these regions.

During this century musk oxen have been successfully transplanted to Norway, Iceland, and Spitsbergen. It is no longer necessary to shoot down a whole herd to separate a few animals from the others and take them to another place. Methods have been developed that will hurt none of them.

Men in helicopters or swift snowmobiles overtake the herd and either lasso or net the animals desired. Then they are quickly hauled away from the others. To keep them from dying of fright or catching pneumonia, they are given injections of mild sedatives and antibiotics. They are then flown to their new homes and released. If the climate and pasturage are right, the animals can take care of themselves.

In 1930 the United States decided to reintroduce the musk ox into Alaska. It bought thirty-four calves and yearlings from Denmark. After capture in Greenland, they were flown across the continent to Alaska and placed on Nunivak Island off the coast. The animals throve there, until by 1968 the herd numbered seven hundred and fifty—too many for the small island. Once again some are being transplanted, this time to the Alaskan mainland, where musk oxen have not walked for more than a century.

Then in 1975 the musk oxen of Nunivak spanned an even greater time gap. At the request of the Soviet Union forty of their number were flown across the Bering Strait to be released in Siberia. Today, after thousands of years, musk oxen are again roaming the ancient home tundras of Eurasia.

Because the Eskimos have such a hard life in the far north, they have learned to put everything possible to use. When the Eskimo women on Nunivak came upon the tufts of musk ox wool (or qiviut, as the Eskimos call it), they began gathering it. They spun it into coarse thread and wove shawls for themselves. They were good shawls because musk ox wool is among the best in the world. It's softer than angora, has sufficient strength, and is easy to work with.

In 1954 Professor John J. Teal, Jr., President-Director of the Institute of Northern Agricultural Research, decided to try domesticating the musk ox and breeding it for its wool. If this could be done it would provide a good livelihood for the impoverished Eskimos. He started raising a few calves on his farm in Vermont. Even though the climate was unfavorable, he was successful enough to realize that it could be done. In 1964 he moved his experimental breeding station to the University of Alaska in Fairbanks.

Today the station has a herd of domesticated musk oxen that is tended by Eskimo herdsmen. When the animals shed their wool the herdsmen peel it off in great sheets of lightly curled fleece. The fleece is sent to Boston, Massachusetts, where it is spun into yarn. The yarn is returned and distributed to villages that have joined the newly formed Musk Ox Producers Cooperative—known as "Oomingmak." The women in the villages knit the yarn into beautiful sweaters, scarfs, stoles, socks, and mittens, which are sold to customers around the world.

Now the Institute of Northern Agricultural Research is setting up more breeding stations in such places as Canada and Norway. And it is hoped that still others will be opened in Greenland and Iceland. Villages around these locations may join Oomingmak to knit qiviut garments for sale.

But this is only the beginning of Professor Teal's dream. Soon he hopes to see the first Alaskan village with its own herd. Little

by little other villages will acquire herds too. Qiviut will become more plentiful and therefore easier and cheaper to buy. And Eskimos who are now living on limited incomes will be able to make a better living.

The musk oxen will fare better too. No matter what the weather conditions, people will always provide them with enough fodder to survive the cruel winters. Cows, no longer living on starvation rations, will bear calves every year, increasing the musk oxen population.

So, by working together, man and musk ox are helping each other to survive in the cold, inhospitable Arctic.

INDEX

ABOUT THE AUTHOR

Margaret Rau was born and grew up in Swatow, China. She came to the United States to attend high school and then returned to China to study the language and classical literature. An extensive traveler, she recently toured the Soviet Union and the People's Republic of China. Ms. Rau is the author of numerous books for both young people and adults and is also a photographer. Her interest in very cold regions led to the study of the musk ox, which she calls "a creature of amazing fortitude, patience, and gentleness." The mother of five children, she now lives in Los Angeles, California.

ABOUT THE ARTIST

Patricia Collins has illustrated many books of a scientific nature and is particularly interested in biology. Over the past years she has become thoughtful of how plants and animals adapt to their environment, and has done over sixty etchings on the subject for her various books. The beautiful aquatint etchings in this book convey the musk ox's indomitable spirit in his lonely habitat. With her family, the artist lives in a converted cranberry factory, which also serves as her studio, in Duxbury, Massachusetts.

Juv
599.735
Rau

WALDOBORO PUBLIC LIBRARY

1916 41949